Saved, Delivered, Healed and Set Free

Humble Witnesses
Of
Transformed Lives In Jesus Christ

Order additional copies of

Saved,

Delivered,

Healed and

Set Free

This book is free!

When ordering, call, fax or email to inquire about shipping costs. All contributions to help defray expenses are gratefully received.

Phone - 1-800-480-1638
Fax - 973-729-6787
loving@lovinggrace.org
www.lovinggrace.org

Saved,

Delivered,

Healed and

Set Free

Humble Witnesses
Of
Transformed Lives In Jesus Christ

© 2012 Loving Grace Ministries
ISBN 978-0-944648-70-4
Library of Congress Control Number: 2012939572

All Scripture quotations, except where otherwise noted, are
taken from the New American Standard Bible, ©1960, 1962,
1963, 1968, 1971, 1972, 1973, 1975, 1977, 1995
by the Lockman Foundation.
Used by permission.

Loving Grace Ministries
PO Box 500
Lafayette, NJ 07848

Figure art - Patti Sullivan

Saved, Delivered, Healed
and Set Free

TABLE OF CONTENTS

Introduction

Saved, Delivered, Healed and Set Free is a sharing of life in letters - real lives, real trials, real suffering, real pain, real loss, real gain, real love, real God, real joy, real new life, real abundance.

These letters of changed lives just may change your life!

Some entries are brief, just a word or two from an individual. Some entries are longer. Some chapters contain multiple letters from the same person - miracles unfolding over time - each step recounting new breakthroughs in healing, understanding and wholeness. In these particular letters the dates are included, showing growth and development over real time. Also, some letters contain their own "unique" punctuation, which has been left in place, to best reflect the emotion and personality of the writer.

Where did these letters come from and why were they written? They come from individuals who have been touched and changed forever by God. They were written to the host of a radio program, "Let's Talk About Jesus" (LTAJ), Wayne Monbleau, who has been "on the air" with LTAJ since 1977 (through Loving Grace Ministries - LGM).

Throughout this book the "fish" symbol is seen. $\propto$ separates letters that are from the same writer, whereas separates authors from each other. The "fish" symbol was an early church "code" sign for true Christian fellowship in the midst of much persecution. The five letters of the Greek word "fish" stand for "Jesus Christ God's Son Savior."

The word, Gospel, means "good news." The good news, the great news represented here in these pages is that God is alive and changing lives - transforming people in broken situations into new creations, turning those who were lost into "found" beloved children of a loving God.

These same transformations which you are about to witness are available, now for you, through the love of God in Jesus Christ. May God truly bless you as you read.

SAVED

Ken

DECEMBER 1, 2009

In December of 2004 my father and mother went to be with the LORD (three days apart). And because of this, and an already severe addiction to drugs, alcohol, and cigarettes, I just about died myself. BUT I KNOW FOR SURE, that I was not on my way to heaven!

I'm a 43 year old Husband and Father who put my family through hell... And after three years of self destruction, I made a new year's resolution to read the BIBLE... You probably thought my resolution was going to be to stop drinking, smoking and doing drugs, BUT I TRIED THAT EVERY YEAR AND FAILED to stop... As a matter of fact it always got worse and worse.

THEN I started reading the BIBLE and before I knew it, I WAS CHANGING ON THE INSIDE, and I wasn't killing myself or hurting my family in the process.

Fast forward to March of 2009, a friend of mine, from work, told me about WLIX, and I tuned in and heard your show "Let's talk about JESUS." I have been a faithful listener ever since. I was SAVED soon after, and have joined A CHRIST CENTERED CHURCH.

I am so grateful to you, and for your teachings. And for helping me to get to know "HIM." JESUS CHRIST IS THE WAY, THE TRUTH AND THE LIFE!!! "HE" has helped me change my evil ways, has shown me the truth about myself and has given me life (eternal). My family really appreciates the "NEW" me, and are all doing well!!! AND MY WIFE LOVES ME AGAIN!!! ALL BECAUSE "HE" LOVES ME...

Yours in CHRIST, ken

∝

DECEMBER 3, 2009

I would like to thank you for your kind WORDS concerning MY TESTIMONY, which you read on the air, Wednesday, December 2nd. I would also like to take this opportunity to add to it, and to fill in some blanks.

I Thank GOD with all my heart, that on Thanksgiving day I celebrated two years sobriety and two years without smoking. Not by my will... but by the will and Saving Grace of MY LORD and SAVIOR JESUS CHRIST (I was saved around Easter 2009).

After I was sober for a year, my then 17 year old daughter gave me A BEAUTIFUL GIFT... a report from school titled "My father, My Hero."

It starts out with how I was a terrible father, who just sat on the porch drinking beer and chain smoking and then went on to say that when her grandparents died, my addictions got worse until I found out that I had diabetes, since I drank everyday and weighed over 300 pounds. And when my Doctor warned me that if I didn't change I'd probably die... "Ever since that day he stopped smoking and drinking and replaced that with dieting and working out. Along with these new changes my dad started to read The Bible." She wrote, "READING THE BIBLE CHANGED HIM COMPLETELY. MY DAD SAID THAT HIS EYES WERE FINALLY OPENED. MY EYES WERE OPENED AS WELL. I no longer viewed my FATHER as the man who sat on the porch drinking and chain smoking. I saw him as my hero."

She goes on to write, "I admire him for his strength, and most of all his ability to change. He inspires me to create goals for myself and to attain them. Because of him, I am motivated to be a better person at everything that I do... He has taught me that people make mistakes, but it is never too late to change and improve."

She then goes on to finish with, "The most important lesson that I have learned from my father is that in order to be successful I must go through life with CLEAR vision because that is the only way to see the world for what it truly is. Now I look at my father in a new light. He will never just be my father; he will forever and always be my hero."

Could you imagine that this BEAUTIFUL CHILD, who I neglected and hurt for all those years, could find it in her heart to forgive me? Like I said in my email, "My wife Loves me again," and by the Grace of

GOD, so does my daughter. I LOVE MY Family so much, and I know how blessed I am, and this would not be possible without the LOVE of JESUS CHRIST!!! On the day I got SAVED... It all became crystal clear, it's not about me!!!

I've gotten involved in a discipleship and a life development class with my CHURCH... and have opened myself up to having a close personal relationship with the LOVER of my Soul.

"Into your hand I commit my Spirit; you have ransomed me, O LORD, GOD of TRUTH" (Psalm 31:5).

*"It is a trustworthy statement, deserving full acceptance, that CHRIST JESUS came into the world to save sinners, among whom I am foremost of all."

"Yet for this reason I found mercy so that in me as the foremost, JESUS CHRIST might demonstrate HIS perfect patience as an example for those who would believe in Him for Eternal life" (1 Timothy 1:15 & 16).

Yours in CHRIST, Ken

* Wayne, On the day you read my testimony you said this Scripture Verse (a couple of times). I don't believe in coincidence, I believe in JESUS CHRIST. By the way, this is MY LIFE SCRIPTURE!

ken

∝

JANUARY 26, 2010

Since being SAVED in March of 2009, time has

appeared to slow down, and what was important prior to SALVATION, now seems to be of less significance. Everything has taken the back seat, and JESUS has taken the wheel.

Every day I find myself being blessed, in some way, shape or form.

JESUS CHRIST has given me a new heart, and He is restoring all the years that the locusts had eaten. "Thanks be to GOD! He gives us the victory through our Lord JESUS CHRIST" (1 Corinthians 15:57).

Yours in Christ, ken

June 2010

The world around us might be rough, and some of the people in it might be in the dark, but they know a "GOOD" thing when they see it!!! I'm a custodian at a local High School, and our normal lunch-time starts at 12 noon, but for the past year or so, I have been the exception to the rule. Since being SAVED in March of 2009, my boss and fellow workers have absolutely no problem with the fact that my lunch-hour starts at 11:30.

As a matter of fact, if we were in the middle of something, and 11:30 is drawing near, my boss and/or fellow workers say, "Hey Ken, it's time for Monbleau and LET'S TALK ABOUT JESUS." I usually hang around to finish the job at hand, but most of the time they tell me to go and listen to the "WORD" and to fill them in about it after lunch. I don't know if they really like to hear the GOOD NEWS" or if they're just being polite, but either way... IT'S ALL GOOD!!!

Yours in Christ, ken

∝

JULY 29, 2010

GOD IS LOVE and JESUS is in my HEART!!!
The world is so void of LOVE, and yet it's the one thing that everyone wants, needs and deserves. How awesome would it be, if all the world could see the LOVE that's inside of me!? Lord open their eyes so they could see what you've done for me!!!

LOVE IS KIND... You shall LOVE the LORD your GOD with all your HEART, and with all your SOUL and with all your MIND. LOVE YOUR NEIGHBOR AS YOURSELF!!! "Dear friends, let us love one another, for love comes from God. Everyone who loves has been born of God and knows God" (1 John 4:7).

I'm Loving Life. What a BLESSING!!!
Yours in Christ, ken

∝

NOVEMBER 30, 2010

I woke up on Thanksgiving morning and I was so grateful when I realized that I was now sober for three years!!! And as I look back on these 3 glorious years, I am amazed at how Amazing HIS Grace is.

I am truly a "new creation" and the LIGHT of the SON is shining so bright in my life, that I can't even see who I used to be when I was in the dark. "Therefore if anyone is in Christ, he is a new creature; the old things are passed away; behold, new things have come" (2 Corinthians 5:17). HALLELUJAH!!!

For the Lord God Almighty, reigns... HE reigns in my heart and HE has given me back the breath that I foolishly blew away. Oh how HE loves me!?!

Even through the trials and tribulations, HE has been a constant provider of peace, love and understanding in my life, and has helped me come out on top in every situation (in HIS time of course).

Even those people who once hated me, now are accustomed to my love, and realize how awesome Jesus is (even though they still lack faith). I can't praise HIM enough, JESUS is everything the Bible says HE is, AND MORE!!! He is being revealed to me each and every glorious day, and Oh how I love HIM!!! I look forward to knowing and growing in HIM always, and forever staying in HIS Word.

HE calls me friend, and that makes me the luckiest man alive... ESPECIALLY when I take into consideration that only three years ago, I was as good as dead, and definitely on the fast track to hell. I was a drug addict, an alcoholic and a chain smoker, and now, since JESUS saved me and broke the curse of addiction, I am the Loving Husband and Father that I was meant to be.

Today is a sad day, because we had to put our 15 year old dog (and best friend) to sleep, and yet... as the Vet gave her a shot that eased her suffering in merely seconds, I just had to thank the Lord for all the years we had with her. And it reinforced my "new" view on life... LIFE is such a precious gift, and instead of taking it for granted, I'm taking advantage of it!!! JESUS CHRIST is the WAY, the TRUTH and the LIFE, and what an awesome life it is!!! THANK YOU JESUS, I LOVE YOU!!!

Yours in Christ, ken

✠

JANUARY 11, 2011

May The Grace Of Our Lord Jesus Christ Be Revealed To Us All Continuously Throughout Each And Every Glorious Day!!!

Today at work, I was talking with my worldly friends about the world and the troubles therein. And of course 2012 came up, and how the world might actually be coming to an end. Especially if you look at all the devastation that is going on throughout the world today, and the horrible things that are happening to the innocent. I told them that only the FATHER knows when that day will come, and then took the opportunity to share the Gospel once again. And no matter how many times I share the "GOOD NEWS" with my long-time friends, they look at me like I'm out of my mind, and they still don't get it... They think that it's about them and their good works and how they're good people and how they're not as bad as the next guy... etc., etc.

I hope that one day they will all know the LOVE

OF JESUS CHRIST!!! I LOVE MY LORD JESUS CHRIST SO MUCH, AND THANK HIM DAILY FOR SAVING ME. I THANK HIM FOR THE CROSS AND FOR TAKING ALL MY SINS UPON HIMSELF. I THANK GOD with all my heart, THAT MY HEAVENLY FATHER CAN ONLY SEE CHRIST IN ME AND NOT WHAT I USED TO BE!!! I am at HIS feet, and I long for the day when I can see HIM face to face... I LOVE MY LORD JESUS CHRIST SO MUCH and I Pray that those whom I love, who are still in the world, might one day get the revelation that only "GOD IS GOOD," and that life without HIM is as bad as it gets!!!

Yours in Christ, ken

May the Grace of our Lord Jesus overflow in your lives.

It's hard to believe that it has only been a little over two years since I first heard about "Let's Talk About Jesus." And it was exactly 2 years ago when I first contacted Loving Grace Ministries and submitted my testimony which Brother Wayne read on the air Dec. 2, 2009. I'M THE GUY WHOSE WIFE LOVES HIM AGAIN!!! After the loss of my parents, and nearly drinking and drugging myself to death, I made a new year's resolution to read the Bible, and Hallelujah, oh how that resolved some of the problems in my life!?! "With men this is impossible, but with God all things are possible"

(Matt. 19:26).

I was a neglectful and hurtful, horrible good for nothing chain smoking drug addict and alcoholic who put my wife and kids through hell, and hurt them more than I would care to admit. They most certainly DID NOT deserve this terrible treatment. As a matter of fact, if anyone on the face of the earth deserved to be in hell, it was me. "But God, who is rich in mercy, because of His great love with which He loved us, even when we were dead in trespasses, made us alive together with Christ (by grace you have been saved), and raised us up together, and made us sit together in the heavenly places in Christ Jesus, that in the ages to come He might show the exceeding riches of His grace in His kindness toward us in Christ Jesus" (Ephesians 2:4-7).

Because HE loved me, and because of His loving kindness towards me, He instantly took away the generational curse of alcoholism (as well as addictions to drugs and cigarettes) and when I was able to see clearly for the first time, I finally realized how much my family meant to me, and how much they were really worth. And in turn, because of the love of Jesus, I became someone worth loving.

On Thanksgiving day of 2007, and almost three years after the loss of my Parents, I was sober and clean for the first time in a long, long time (I was 10 years old when I started using alcohol and 12 years old when I started using drugs... sad but true). It's weird, when I look at 10 and 12 year old kids today, I can't remember ever being that young. Because of drugs and alcohol, I missed out on being a kid, but I didn't truly become a man until I got Born Again (at 43 years old).

Now I'm sober for four years, and I enjoy being

a responsible grown up.

I realize what an awesome gift life is, and how very precious are the ones I love!!!

My family has forgiven me, and Jesus Christ is doing great things in my life. And if you could find a man who loves his wife and kids more than I do, I'm sure he has Christ in his life as well.

He has definitely made this middle aged man a new creation.

"So then faith comes by hearing, and hearing by the word of God" (Romans 10:17). Grace to all those who love our Lord Jesus Christ.

ken

2

DELIVERED
From Addiction

Tommy

DECEMBER 29, 2009

I write this letter having almost no income, no permanent job and am one month away from losing my apartment - but not without hope!

I reflect on how God, through His body - specifically LGM - has given me hope for 25 years in the darkest times when all seemed hopeless. 25 years ago, after being newly saved, and freed from addiction, all that was told to me was that I must work, work, work, for a holy God that did me a favor 2000 years ago and now expects payback big time from me.

Hearing this message I felt hopeless - until I listened to LTAJ for the first time. There I heard about Jesus as He really was. I was told that Jesus died for me because He loved me and wanted me to know Him - and that He was willing to go to any length - even to give His life - that I might know how much He loves me. I remember hearing about grace for the first time - being the very essence of God - and how God's salvation couldn't be earned, it was a gift freely given to me by God. I'll never forget that day when a burden was lifted from my heart and I was given assurance deep within my spirit - the only way I can verbalize it is that I was given hope.

Several years later, after sharing that hope with anyone I could grab hold of, but not spending any time alone with Jesus, and not having any discipline in my life, I backslid. I relapsed back into active addiction.

For 18 years I allowed sin and the enemy to dictate to me who God was and who I was. I became a heroin addict, at times lived in parks, compromised everything I believed in to get the next fix, enslaved completely to addiction.

Throughout those 18 years I hated myself. I hated God, and hated people. I lived in a relationship with an unbeliever who wanted nothing to do with Jesus and had 2 sons with her. I overdosed more times than I could count, was arrested several times, and lived in complete humiliation and degradation. The only prayer I could pray was for death. I believed I was a cast-off, a reprobate, doomed forever, never to feel the light of God's love in my heart.

But there was one hour throughout 6 days a week, when I could listen to LTAJ, and something happened in that hour - in the midst of my sin and pain - that I can't adequately explain in words, but hope sprang up in my heart, hope that maybe Jesus still loved me and would free me from my chains.

Almost 4 years ago, I was in a bathroom on the lower east side of Manhattan; I injected myself with heroin and began to die. I fell to my knees, saw my life pass before me and with my last gasping breath I surrendered to Jesus from my heart. At that moment, breath came back into my lungs, and I was able to stand. I was no longer intoxicated. After I left that place, hope began to return to my heart more frequently.

I went into a detox, and people I believe were sent directly from the Lord gave a message of hope and freedom that I could really be free from active addiction and find a new way of life. In the detox in Seabrook, NY, while in the middle of the unbearable pain of withdrawal, I turned on my little transistor radio - on a Sunday - and again heard Wayne's voice amazingly speaking to me about how God is with me in the midst of my pain. I responded to God's loving call, like the prodigal son. I began to read the Bible again and seek the Lord. My therapist in the secular detox was a believer and ministered to me daily.

As soon as I left the detox, I contacted you and let you know everything, and you prayed for me. Not long after that my younger son Daniel got saved. I returned to my church home that had prayed for me for years.

My hope and my dream for 25 years was to attend worship in the woods [LGM Retreat Weekend], to worship with other believers freely and to share the kindness and mercy the Lord had shown me in my life through LGM. There I was able to recommit my life and be baptized. By God's grace I was able to maintain close ties to my sons, and this past year my son Daniel attended WIW with me and was baptized.

Since being brought back to the Lord, He has given me a ministry to work with people that suffer with addiction. Several of these have come to Him. I asked God for a partner in ministry. He answered my prayer and I met the most beautiful woman I have ever seen and together we minister to sick and suffering addicts, endeavoring to bring them to Christ. Recently a young man named Phil with no religious indoctrination who had never been to church, gave his heart to Jesus after being prayed for.

I said all this to say to you and to all in similar circumstances, that it's always darkest before the dawn. Today for me, hope doesn't necessitate outward signs, but a deep trust that God is able to supply all our needs according to His riches in glory in Christ Jesus.

I can't thank enough all who through their support and prayers made this miracle of my life possible. If not for this ministry, I would probably be just a statistic of another dead junkie, with an unmarked grave in a potter's field. But, instead, despite my circumstances, I am filled with hope and faith that God will see me through these rough times because of the hope and assurance He has given me.

As a result of God's grace, <u>today I have 3 years, 11 months and 7 days clean</u> - and I am graced to share this daily in the 12 step meetings I attend - when I think on that I am filled with joy and gratitude for God and I know anything is possible.

Love, Tommy

JULY 7, 2010

I'm writing this letter to express my gratitude to

our Lord, for all that's been done in my life. I don't know where to start. It's so rare to see and hear Jesus, and Jesus alone, lifted up and His love and mercy proclaimed.

A little over 27 years ago I gave my life to Christ. Jesus revealed Himself to me just before I was ready to commit suicide.

All I had known prior to my experience with our Lord was violence, abuse and fear. I dreaded every day I had to live on this planet.

When I turned my heart and my will over to Jesus' loving care; love, joy and peace began to permeate my whole being. This was overwhelming.

I was attending a part of the body of Christ whose focus wasn't Jesus, but works and service. The Jesus they spoke of wanted results, and right away, and my value to Him was based upon this philosophy. These teachings robbed me of my love and joy and peace that I had received at the moment of my salvation.

In my heart of hearts I knew that the Jesus they were talking about wasn't the Jesus I met. But I was afraid - what if I was wrong? What if this was too good to be true, what if the Jesus I had met was a figment of my imagination and this was the real Jesus? I was conflicted and torn.

Then one day a brother told me about your program. I can't even describe with words the relief and joy that once again filled my spirit as you shared about Jesus - exactly the way He was when I met Him. You shared that He wasn't uptight about my works, but loved me unconditionally. It wasn't about what I did, but what He had done before the foundation of the world.

Several years had passed and I gave place to

compromise and sin in my life. After a wounding of my heart in a failed relationship, instead of turning to Jesus to walk with me through the feelings of rejection and abandonment, I turned to drugs to medicate these feelings, hoping they would go away. I walked away from Jesus, I backslid, and my life became 7 times worse than it was before coming to know Christ. I became a hopeless heroin addict doing whatever I had to do to get the next fix. For some reason, as hopeless as my existence was, and even though I believed Jesus had given up on me, I still listened to LTAJ daily. When I heard you speak of Jesus, Who He was, in those hour programs, I had hope that maybe, just maybe, this didn't have to end in my death. I went through this for 18 horrible years, hurting God, myself and others on a regular basis - completely enslaved - mind, body and soul, by the merciless, cruel chains of addiction.

During this time I had 2 sons with a woman out of wedlock, was arrested several times, sometimes lived in parks, and prayed for death every day. God would not allow me to die.

I had an experience in a pharmacy bathroom on the lower east side of Manhattan a little over 4 years and 4 months ago, where I injected myself with heroin, and began to die - consciously while I was awake. I had overdosed many times before but I had never had this experience being aware and being awake. As I gasped for breath I fell to my knees. In a moment all my life passed before me, and remarkably my death, and the effect it would have on my sons. I cried from my heart - "Jesus I surrender." Jesus interrupted my death, in fact I was no longer in an altered state of consciousness.

Not long after that, by God's grace, I went into a secular detox program and God had Christians waiting for me on the inside, sharing with me that the Lord still loved me. <u>Today I have 4 years, 4 months, and 2 weeks clean</u>.

Thirty days after I left the detox, I began to attend a part of the Body of Christ that loved me, loved Jesus and loved people. I attended a 12 step program and listened to LTAJ daily. It took *a very long time* to feel like a human being again. But Jesus held me by the hand through the agony of 9 months of withdrawal. During much of those 18 years I held on to one hope - I wanted to attend Worship in the Woods - clean, free and loving Jesus.

Since the Lord brought me back to Himself, I've been able to attend several Worship in the Woods, and experienced the beauty of believers coming together to worship Him in spirit and in truth. The part of the body that I attend started a recovery ministry that I became a part of, along with the 12 step program that I attend. As a result, several members of this 12 step program have become brothers and sisters in Christ. They're doing the same thing now too - sharing the love of Jesus.

About a year and a half ago, I was given another gift from God through LGM. The Lord gave me a special friend and also a helper, who lifts me up like no one else can, as we reach out to others in this broken, dying world, to share the love of Jesus with. And I'm forever grateful.

At Worship in the Woods my son Daniel and myself have been baptized and refreshed by the living waters of the living Christ. Recently my son Shane also received Jesus as His Lord and Savior.

I'm forever grateful for your love for Jesus - and for getting out of the way and letting God do "His" thing. Because of the words of hope you gave me daily, I give hope to hopeless addicts today - in Jesus' name.

Forever grateful, sincerely and prayerfully, Your brother and friend from Staten Island, Tommy

I was introduced to your ministry 25 years ago and I knew in my heart that this is Who I always knew God to be but was afraid to believe it. After hearing the true Gospel, I embraced Jesus for Who He is (not for who I thought He was, or who people told me He is); love personified.

Prior to hearing your radio program I heard a lot of mixed messages from misinformed people pulling Scriptures out of context about a God who wanted obedient slaves to do His will out of guilt, shame, and fear of judgement and punishment, and if they didn't like it, they could burn in hell forever. This God shown to me was angry, resentful and full of wrath for His creation's inherent sinfulness. This God was out to prove He was God and that was that! This God scared me so much I wished I wasn't born or wished I didn't exist. I almost had empathy with Lucifer's decision to rebel against a God so cruel.

Then I saw Jesus, and the Father and the Holy Spirit for who God is, not this distorted, twisted version of sinful man's own fears and resentments projected on to the true God (not without Satan's help).

Then I heard you say God's will wasn't for any to perish but for all to come to repentance - that Jesus was humble of heart, and gentle, and offers me rest - that He died for me because He loves me - REALLY loves me - and wants me to know His love and return it to Him and others. I was told life would be hard, but His joy is my strength; His peace my peace, His life my life, His resurrection, my power!

I fell in love with the True Jesus and began to grow. I told others about Him and they came to know Him, and then I put service before Him and my time alone dwindled down to none. I was rejected by a potential girlfriend and I made a decision to walk away from our Lord's care, and I took my will back. Before getting saved I had used drugs and when I was born again God had removed my desire to use drugs. I began to get high again and backslid. I used drugs to cover the pain of the rejection I experienced instead of allowing Jesus to walk me through it.

I became a heroin addict seven times worse than before I had come to Jesus. I lived to use heroin and used heroin to live. I did anything to get my next shot. I was enslaved over and over again in body, mind and spirit. Every day my prayer was for death, and I hated Jesus for cursing me (or so I thought). My life was spent overdosing, living on park benches, jails, robbing and lying. I became like an animal. I lived for survival alone.

All I thought about was heroin. I was obsessed and enslaved, filled with guilt and shame. Every day at 11:30 for whatever reason, unless I was without batteries or in a jail, I listened, and for the 60 minutes I was given something priceless - hope. Hope that I could get clean and that Jesus still loved me and had a plan for my life. After the program I would return to the horrors of active addiction, but you gave me for 18 years a reason not to blow my brains out. In those 60 minutes I felt peace and hope that God had not given up on me.

Then a little over 5 years ago I shot up in a bathroom in a pharmacy in the lower east side of NYC, and I began to die, awake. I felt my life passing before my eyes and my life ending as just another junkie in Potter's Field. I cried out to Jesus for another chance. I surrendered to His Lordship.

I went into a 30-day secular rehab and it was there I renewed my relationship with Jesus and after 30 days I began to attend 12 step meetings. I went through 9 months of horrible withdrawals, but Jesus was with me and I trusted Him. My church family also supported me and received me as if I had never sinned. It was my dream to attend Worship in the Woods clean, and since, I've been to several winter retreats also.

Two years ago I prayed for God's will for a mate, and I met her, and recently we were engaged. She also has a heart for addicts who still suffer without recovery and without Christ. Since surrendering I have seen my sons come to Christ and watched many addicts receive Him and begin to respond to His love and call.

I'm clean for 4 years, 11 months and 3 days. Every day is a miracle, and all I see is the miracle when I watch God do for others what He's done for me! I am renewed, transformed and rejoicing for all God has done in my life; not only in my life, but in the lives of every addict I can tell.

I have a life I only dreamed of having. God is Love. Love, Tommy from Staten Island

Gina

Grace and peace to you and yours. Just have to - once again - give Glory to God for all the goodness and grace that has come into my life.

I couldn't fully describe all the ways in which God has used your program to guide, direct, encourage and give words of Life and hope through times of soaring on eagle's wings - as well as in the deepest depths of darkness.

I have struggled with life and as a Christian. Early in my walk with the Lord I was seduced by a cult and almost threw it all away - that was the first time God spoke to me personally through your broadcast. I found God near and present in a way that dissolved all the doubt and twisted darkness that came to me in the way of guilt and self condemnation. God was leading me to light and life and truth - God was alive and well outside the walls of that group in ways I never knew in my small personal prison. Truly He came to me and set the captive free.

Prior to this time I had struggled with addiction - in various forms - once having had an accidental overdose from drugs. Later the root of the addiction came through in other controlling, compulsive behaviors. Even within Christianity and serving the Lord these behaviors surfaced - as I "burnt-out serving the Lord." Sad but true. Another time it all almost crashed and burned - but you were there on the radio and I heard God showing me ways to find healing and balance through a Christ-centered life of prayer and worship. The worship retreats, seminars and services were always havens of grace - encouraging and strengthening me to keep on keeping on with Jesus - one day at a time step by step into all the ways He - not I - would have in store.

All those years are too much to chronicle - but God has been faithful through grief and pain, loss and confusion. In the past few years, I have found much help and growth through 12 step-recovery and contemplative prayer, the latter came through exposure to the Desert Fathers and classics of the faith I was encouraged to explore by your teachings in past years.

Once on a retreat I was encouraged by a priest to pray for other addicts like myself-- which began a practice that stands to this day. Around this time I also felt God leading me to take more serious action toward ministry. I wasn't sure about seminary - but through a couple years of prayer and counsel I entered seminary in an urban ministry program in Philadelphia.

Just after this decision - on one of your LGM Worship in the Woods retreats - I heard a story of an addict that moved me toward more prayer and action. At your following fall retreat - in 2008 - I met the recovering addict whose story I had heard only a few months prior. We met briefly when I decided to let him know I had been praying for him. Two months later he invited me to his church community outreach - this began a relationship that has put us two recovering addicts together in ways that God would use to help reach out to other troubled lives - many whose stories are riddled with addiction - and many are finding grace.

And grace upon grace, this year we plan to marry! How much more can one ministry give to one life? Truth is

- I'm certain my life would have never took the twists and turns it had to endure without the help and support of God coming to me through LGM.

From an 18 year old lost and hopeless kid - to now a 43 year old woman planning to complete seminary and to marry the man God brought through your ministry! What else can I say but to praise God and give thanks.

For all that has been, thanks. For all that will be, yes.

And may much more fruit continue to abound. Much love and gratitude, Gina

Tommy and Gina
wed July 21, 2012

Karen

OCTOBER 15, 2009

I need help. I am looking to become closer to MY Father and his Son JESUS, more than ever now.

I was a drug addict for 22 years of my life, but God did for me what I could not do for myself -- I was blinded by evil, my children were taken from me by the state, my marriage was over, and I was nothing but an empty shell. Far from the spiritual little girl I had always been... I put myself into a recovery program, and cleaned up very well. During the first months of my sobriety... I listened to WFIL (phila. area). That radio was my life, and many nites... YOU put me to sleep.

I love Let's Talk About Jesus, and I want to express my gratitude. I still am very active in my recovery, and have been clean for two years now (just celebrated on Oct. 10, 2009). There is still much pain in my life and fear rears its ugly head from time to time---but God in me is greater than any evil force on the Earth, and YOU taught me that!!!

I know that I am forgiven, for I should be dead doing the past things I did, being in very dangerous places w/people who had no regard for a blessing called life.

Pray for me that I may find strength to keep believing in myself, help other women who suffer from what I went through, and walk always w/God... may we take the path of Truth and Light always. I am saved - but feel far away from the Holy Ghost alot. Please again pray for me. God bless you. You make a difference

Karen.

It is my honest hope and wish that you will read this aloud on the radio one fine day.

My name is Karen and I am a recovered drug addict. I lost my home, marriage, custody of my 3 beautiful children, and became a walking monster w/no soul within me. I did ugly things in ugly places w/some ugly people. And I know what it is to live like you're in hell on earth!!

But, Jesus has saved me! Now I shine (I'm still human, so I'm not perfect) but what God has done for me cannot be conceived in a non-religious soul or mind. I don't think about yesterday, for it is over and my experiences were mapped out by my God for me to seek Him.

Now, I see only blessings rather than bad. I seek to love rather than to be loved, and to understand, rather than to be understood!! I am very active in my recovery program and just celebrated 2 years clean and sober, and I see life thru a "new pair of glasses." I want anyone listening to know that Jesus is there. He will hear you if you beg His mercy and pray through Christ to our Father.

I fell to the floor in all the tears I could produce that fine day I gave up the drugs... and spoke to my God through Jesus, and gave up my life, along with my efforts. I am now living the life that God intended Karen to live when I was born.

All those who suffer from addiction... go get help and take God's Hand, miracles do happen! I'm one of them, and I do my best to give it back today by speaking about it.

Karen

Philly

I come from a place where the only time I had ever heard God's name was as profanity and maybe in a movie. I come from a place of sexual and drug abuse, looking for acceptance from anyone and everything, and continually expanding the void by trying to fill it with everything but The One Thing that would fill it, and never being aware of what was really missing.

The word "God" was literally never mentioned in my house growing up, as my father was agnostic and my mother a non-practicing Catholic completely removed from an already distant faith. I come from a place where I was sexually abused and handed the works of existentialist writers, given different medications, different therapists, and countless clinical and cold solutions that put more emphasis on self-reliance and dependence on the world. I welcomed the use of drugs into my life as a legitimate lifestyle and means to an end.

Until the summer of last year, I had only heard the words "Jesus Christ" used as an expletive, and never gave God, religion, faith, etc. any attention as my existence was completely self absorbed.

I began "looking for Him" out of desperation when I had about 6 months clean and was demanding that the universe show me something real.

In this desperation, it was suggested to me to simply ask God to reveal Himself to me. Slowly, simply, and gently He began to draw me near to Him in ways that, still to this day, will only make sense if you've lived inside my head my entire life. I identify so much with a heart being softened, a veil being lifted, scales falling from my eyes, and seeing that I was being sought after, that I had no idea who I was, what was truly going on around me, and what reality was at all.

I experienced not a reformation but a transformation and began my walk with new lungs, new feet, new eyes, a new tongue, a new heart; all of which weren't mine, but at the same time, were absolutely mine. I've experienced what it's like to be used as an instrument, what it's like to fall painfully short, and all the while be reminded simply by the ministry of Loving Grace of just that - His loving grace.

I pray that this message will continue to be spread and serve as the catalyst for growth in the Spirit that it has been for me. Thank you for the consistency, the simplicity, the fellowship, and reminding me to seek the still, small voice that I could never hear before.

Philly

Michael

February 2, 2010

It was 1986 when I started listening to your radio show in Philadelphia. At the time I was a year clean in narcotics anonymous. That year I rented a 6 bedroom house in Jenkintown, a suburb of Phila. I rented rooms to other clean addicts in N.A.

We all listened to your show and bought your tapes. I still have dozens of them. Your tapes were a huge help to us, in working the 12 steps, being that the 12 steps are spiritual principles. Like, the 1st step is acceptance, acceptance of the truth. Step 2 - faith, step 3 - commitment/unconditional love.

Your tape on acceptance was one we all listened to over and over. We all practiced acceptance of ourselves, reality, and others through spiritual surrender, not fighting. Your tape on faith was another instrumental tape, and we learned that the way to practice our new found (small amount) of faith was by saying "THANK YOU" to our higher power. Your tape on gratitude was another big help. We found through our experience of working steps 1 and 2, acceptance and faith through surrender and gratitude, that our lives began to change and we lost the desire to use, and found we were all filled with hope from working the 1st step. And by working the 2nd step we were filled with joy, and this led us to commitment, in the 3rd step, and we practiced this commitment through service. As members of N.A., we tried to carry this message of hope, that other addicts could get this message of hope, and lose the desire to use.

Well, I could talk about all that kind of stuff for hours, but the reason I was writing was to say that your ministry was such a big influence on us. You see, N.A. was started in Philadelphia in 1972, but up until 1985 it had, at most, 10 or 15 meetings, and almost folded a few times, with no meetings in the north or west Phila.

But nobody ever worked the steps or knew how.

It was not until myself and those guys I lived with, along with a few others, that we started an N.A. group called "for addicts only" and we started to incorporate spiritual principles in our lives, along with a conscience effort on group principles, the 12 traditions.

We started having a group conscience meeting once or twice a month where we prayed together and asked God to guide us as a group to carry the message.

It was at this point that N.A. changed forever in Philadelphia, where for 14 years N.A. struggled to survive with around a dozen meetings. Well, within the next 3 years we had over 200 new meetings. The Spirit of Truth came into our group and people came from all over and our example did the rest. All the members of that group were avid listeners to "Let's Talk About Jesus."

Michael

P.S. 12 members of that group came to see you share back in the 1980's. It was a big deal to us to see you back then. All 12 who came to see you that day are all still members of N.A. We all are still clean, and we all are productive members of society.

3

POWER IN THE NAME OF JESUS

Teresa

My father died when I was twenty two years old. I am now forty years old.

My father and I would listen to you. He looked forward to hearing you on the radio and I did too. It was precious time spent with my father.

He told me that there was power in the name of Jesus. He told me to call upon The Lord Jesus if I ever found myself in harm's way. "Jesus will help you" he said with tears in his eyes. I wasn't sure why he cried at the time, but I had a sense that, in time, I would understand.

Time passed and I was in harm's way. With a gun to my head, attacked in an elevator. I couldn't move, I was so terrified, and the conversation with my father, when we listened to you on the radio years prior all came to me.

The only word that came out of my mouth was JESUS.

A miracle happened right at that moment and I am alive today to say THANK YOU!

I thank God for you.

Teresa

4

HEALED
God's Healing Love

Anonymous

I remember, it was the New Year... I was in terrible shape... I had backslidden after my husband left me... I had horrible relationships with men... it was one right after the other... I was feeling so low and I decided to listen to LTAJ during my lunch hour... My mother was a longtime listener; she got me listening too.

Anyway... I was sitting in my car... my self esteem was at an all time low... and I was trying to find love in men... I remember... Wayne got on the radio and said, "You become what you behold."

I cried my eyeballs out... because I saw my state... how far away from Christ I was.

I am crying now thinking about it... but that changed my life that day.

I decided there that I was turning back to Christ and wanted to behold **HIM** and nothing else.

Well here I am... knowing how He has healed me.

It's been a tough journey back but it's been worth the fight!

And now I am going to be ministering to women who are doing what I did and to encourage them to put Christ back on the throne of their heart where He belongs.

I just want to say THANK YOU because of that word... I was able to give my life back to Jesus! Now I give back to others what was given to me.

Anonymous

Marilyn

I have to let you know that within these last three weeks you have taught me what has been missing from my "walk" with the Lord. Maybe I'm not alone.

I've been missing out on the relationship with Him. Even though I could make a long list of stuff related to Christianity, I never did them out of the amazing undeserved LOVE He has for me.

This is huge.

It's melted my heart like nothing else can.

I feel like I did when I first got saved some 25 years ago. I want to love everyone through the Love flowing through me.

I must confess that I've also repented of not submitting to His LORDSHIP in many areas of my heart. The ugly stuff that's so well hidden. Convicted not condemned!

I have also been in the Gospel of John. It's alive and can never get "learned" fully. I encourage my brothers and sisters, never assume you've "read" already. Be encouraged to continue in His mission, first to know His love and then to share it!!!!!

I see and hear so differently now. Praise Him!
Marilyn

Jackie

The Lord has spoken many times in many ways over the years, but there was one word one day which spoke to the core of my being in reference to "a thorn" of affliction with which I have been challenged the last 29 years.

Someone called in about being diagnosed bipolar. Wayne, you replied that if someone was genuinely diagnosed bipolar, that even with that challenge in their life, they would be able to live the abundant life Jesus came to give us! Thank you Lord and Let's Talk About Jesus.

Jesus used that call as a turning point and has brought transformation in me.

Now, when I get to the point where I don't know what to do, I ask the Lord, "Lord, what do you want me to do?" He always says, "Calmly, rest in my arms while I take care of you."

What a good Shepherd Jesus is. You'll never know the gratitude in my heart for the love of Christ poured into my life that day.

Jackie

Felícia

There was a time in my life when I fell into sin. The guilt I felt was unbearable. I cried out to God in repentance.

Then you had a message about God's forgiveness and it freed me from my guilt. You speak the words of Jesus, "your sins are forgiven."

Recently a man called who had O.C.D. You said today everything is given a title. Years ago there was no name for O.C.D. or A.D.D. Now everything is given three letters. Years ago this man would not have been labeled O.C.D. People were just considered peculiar.

Whatever <u>we</u> have, give it to God. God's grace is sufficient. I am a <u>child</u> of <u>God</u>. Take it to God. What may be a negative to people may be special to God.

Those words healed me and freed me of the guilt I had felt.

God is faithful.

Your sister in Christ, Felicia

Winifred

I have been born again since 1975 and have attended a number of different churches and have intently studied the Bible, spoke in tongues, received wisdom (personally - not the type where you get up in a church and shout it out) - received healings and seen God work tremendously miraculously in my life so many, many times.

But the older I got, I realized I was actually becoming more afraid of God, not more secure. I wrongly attributed this to aging.

When I first started listening to you on the radio about a year ago, my attitude was, "Boy this guy sure talks about Jesus a lot - way too much for my tastes."

Although I continued to listen to you on the way home from work everyday, I could never quite understand this passion of Jesus. Yes, I seemed to center mainly on having the Holy Spirit and going directly to God the Father with all my heart's issues - Jesus had done His part on the cross, I had accepted this and that was that as far as His purpose went (I thought).

As the years went by and I experienced the loss of loved ones, a fear was taking root inside of me. I felt like I really didn't know what God was going to put me through next to "teach me something." The thing was, all this time I was in communication with Him and He would offer many, many words of comfort both through the Bible and in my heart, answer prayers, guide and protect me. It's not like we were estranged from one another. But I was still becoming fearful, I just didn't trust like I used to when I was younger.

Recently my 22 year old daughter was diagnosed

with what possibly could turn into a precancerous condition. It wasn't precancerous, but something that should be watched. Most likely her body would overcome it and it would just clear up on its own. This was not the worst news in the world, but it sent me over the edge. It came right on the heels of my mother-in-law and father-in-law passing, my uncle passing and my beloved father passing. I honestly didn't know if I could "trust" God for her to be fine and I entered into prayer about it, being 100% honest with God about my feelings. I learned very early on in my walk with Him to never try to pull any punches with Him about how I felt - just give it all to Him, the good and the bad.

It was while I was in a fearful and basically doubtful prayer, that I was asked, "Do you trust God the Father to take care of your daughter?" And I had to answer, "I'd like to, but, no, I really don't." I was asked "Why?" I answered, "Because He's so exacting. I never know if He's going to decide to heal or not. Or if He's going to teach me a 'lesson.' I'm getting fearful of Him."

Then the voice asked me something that changed my life! I was asked, "Do you trust Jesus to take care of your daughter?" And it's like my eyes were opened. A warmth came flooding over me and I responded with a resounding, "Yes, absolutely! He never says no to anyone. He loves everyone so much!" And I was told, "He is the One that you come to. He is the One that you deal with." It was like a fog was cleared away. I instantaneously saw more clearly than I had seen before and I knew, didn't guess, He loved me.

I was thrilled beyond measure! I "know" Jesus, I "know" His love. I "know" how He dealt and deals with people - Him I know and I don't guess or worry about how He will answer. I've read all about Him over and over, yet somehow I was trying to get to God by going around Him (using His name, but not really acknowledging Him personally)... I can't say enough.

I can't quite explain the transformation, because I have walked with God for 34 years. And my life has not been wrapped up in going to church and being involved and thinking I was walking with God by serving in church - it wasn't like that - I always had a much more personal relationship. We've communed all these years, but I didn't quite "get it."

Now I know exactly what you're talking about when you go on and on about Jesus - and I can't get enough! My whole being loves Him and He loves me and I don't doubt it or question it for a single second. And He loves my kids even more than I do. I am in awe over Him and all He has done. It really is all about Jesus!

No one can come to the Father except right through Him - and what a great way to go - He's just so loving! I can't say enough.

With love and gratitude, Winifred

Argentina

I have a wonderful testimony about God's healing power in the 21st century, praise His Holy Name. I called the radio program and asked for prayer a month ago for my granddaughter who was in intensive care after an overdose of pills. She was in critical condition. The doctors did everything they could. There was no change for almost three weeks. Then I called you and you and me and the rest of our brothers and sisters listening to the program prayed for her and Our Mighty God heard our prayer and healed her.

A few days later she started to get better. Her lungs had filled with blood and fluid and she was on a ventilator, then they had to put a trach in her throat. She spent 45 days in the hospital and now she's home. Her name is Taisha Ramos.

She is completely healed.

Hallelujah! Praise His Holy Name.

Your sister in Christ Jesus, Argentina

Tara

I have been listening to your program since the age of 15, when a Catholic friend introduced me to you.

Having accepted the Lord at the age of 4, being raised in a broken Christian home, something compelled me to listen over and over to the strange, foreign teaching of the totally free love of Jesus.

I kept listening.

Many breakthroughs later, His love has transformed my life, from one of confusion and instability to one built on the solid, unchanging grace and mercy of our

Lord. I am 41 now and I am still listening! Your teachings have helped me to stay focused over the years. There are so many distractions and distortions of God out there! But praise God you are still here, 26 years later, faithfully lifting up the true Lord Jesus Christ.

A few years ago, God used you to put a call out over the radio. I was listening while at work while the radio became very static-y. Something told me to pay attention, listen carefully. I heard you calling believers to serve the Lord, to give their lives to ministry.

Tears fell as I felt the love of God calling me back.

I had given up on my calling years before after several painful emotional/mental afflictions that were holding my life back. Several years later of therapy and treatment and here was God calling me back!

He raised that dream from the dead through your program.

I cannot express the amount of joy and hope I have experienced in serving Him with my life. Thank you for all you have done to proclaim our Lord and to follow Him.

Tara

5

THE BOOK

Diane

On one of your programs years ago, you suggested a book called "The God Of All Comfort" by Hannah Whithall Smith. At the time, I read it on and off periodically and treasured its words.

With the craziness of events of life getting to me, it affected my physical health, and my job at work was getting worse.

One day, my neighbor called me wondering why I was home from work. I told her I wasn't feeling well in spite of doctors, meds, tests, etc. She offered any help I might need.

During the evening I was reading that book for some comfort, since the pain was becoming unbearable. I suddenly started passing and vomiting blood and passing out time and again. I was too weak and out of it to call my neighbor, Lori, for help.

I mustered enough energy to throw the book at the adjoining apartment wall to get her attention.

She heard the "God Of All Comfort" bang on her wall and knew I was in trouble and called the police and ambulance and I was hospitalized for a week. That book and Lori, and of course, Jesus, saved my life.

A year later, in 1996, the Lord prompted me to move to Florida, where, at that time, 3 of my 4 children had moved to and where my grandchildren were being born.

When I said goodbye to Lori, she gave me a gold charm of an angel, as I called her an angel for saving my life. I signed my treasured "God of All Comfort" book and gave it to her, and moved.

On my first Christmas in Florida, a woman I knew, who knew nothing about my experience with Lori and "the book," bought me a copy of "The God of All Comfort" for Christmas. When I thought of all the hundreds of books in a Christian book store, and she chose that one, all I could think of was, "Isn't that just like our God."

I have had a miraculous recovery over these past 13 years in Florida, enjoying the children and grandchildren and am so grateful.

Last year, Lori's husband passed away unexpectedly, leaving her with a teen and a 5 year old. I called her to try in any way to comfort her as she did me. She said she's doing better, and hanging on to and reading, "The God of All Comfort" book. Praise God.

You can't possibly know how many times your words on the air, transform a life. Look what the mention of one book could accomplish!! Thank you again.

Miracle of miracles, at 76, I'm learning the computer in Florida and after 10 years of missing "Let's Talk About Jesus," I've been hearing you again on my laptop. Praise God. And your message is still, Keep Your Eyes on Jesus.

Diana

6

SET FREE

David

I remember when I first got saved. It was back in June 6th of 1982. I was only 21 years old and it was so exciting.

I was so in love with the Lord. I just wanted to sing all the time and bless the Lord. I was also so hungry for His Word, that I would read for hours, because I wanted to know more of Him and what He did in me. At work they called me Moses because I would share about Jesus.

But all that changed as I started going to church and began listening to the wrong messages. As a young Christian I started struggling in my walk with the Lord, and became confused and frustrated, because of all the messages that would always point me to my sin and my failures; all the messages about the laws and rules to follow; all the messages of works and performance.

I would leave feeling guilty and shameful, thinking I'm not doing good enough, that I have to try better. I felt so condemned, feeling like I let the Lord down again.

There were weeks where I didn't even partake of the communion service because I didn't seem worthy enough. There were times where I just stopped seeking God and walked away. But I knew I had nothing better in life than Him and would repent and recommit my life to Christ again. But only to be bombarded with the same messages again from preachers who have what you may call a sin mentality, a works mentality and a law mentality. All that just led me in a downward spiral again.

This went on for a couple of years.

But when the Lord connected me to Loving Grace Ministries, I started listening to "Let's Talk About Jesus" and my world was turned around again, but for the good.

I was hearing more about Jesus and His grace and that blew me away. I started to hear about the love of God, and His goodness to me, and that blessed me so. I went on to also read the book, "Friendship With God" and I couldn't believe that God actually wanted to get that close to me, but He did! Another beautiful revelation was hearing about how we are priests unto the Lord, to minister unto Him, because God wants to bless us with Himself.

All the things that I was so excited about when I first got saved were beginning to all come back again, and I was just loving the Lord like never before. The joy of the Lord was flooding my soul, and I just wanted to sing to Him and bless Him.

It's been a long journey. Thanks for sharing with me the beautiful message that has kept me on a good path for all these years. Just hearing about Who Jesus is and what He has done and all Jesus shares with us is enough for now and forever. You can't go wrong when you share the Truth (Jesus our Truth).

"And you will know the Truth, and the Truth will make you free" (John 8:32).

David

Steven

Your teaching of being Christ-centered has helped me so much.

I have been listening to Let's Talk About Jesus since 1987 just shortly after coming to the Lord. My walk had been off and on through those years.

I had fallen away. For more than 15 years I had walked away from the Lord. But at times I had turned to your ministry to renew my walk.

The Lord had me in the wilderness for those years as Moses was. But now the Lord has spoken to me from the burning bush!!

About two years ago He led me back to Him and now I am stronger in Him than ever before, because I have finally made Him the center of my life!!

It's because of the simple message of Jesus, Jesus, Jesus. He is the Truth, the Light, the Way!! He is now leading me to teach the Word and minister to the lost in the church, and in the world who have put things about Jesus before Jesus!!

He has taken so many false teachings from me and opened my eyes. We must speak the truth in love!! The church is off the tracks when it is self-centered instead of Christ-centered.

Thank you!! You have talked about Jesus all these years and it is a blessing to me!!

His sheep hear His voice!!

Steven

Judy

I was in an almost intolerable crisis of faith. Even though I belong to a great faithful church, I needed daily help, and your program was what was needed.

I could not see God's love for me and I couldn't forgive myself for my life of sin.

But your simple message of Christ's sacrifice for forgiveness of my sin convicted my soul and got me through. I heard the Shepherd's voice through your program and now I'm free.

The Holy Spirit through this ministry is saving lives for Jesus. I know this, because He saved mine.

Love, a bond servant of our Lord Jesus, Judy

Laurie

A few weeks ago on November 12th your program changed my life for the better. Permit me to explain.

I have <u>hated</u> one of my sisters my entire life. I remember hating her when I was 3 years old and I am now 46. So, what happened?

Almost 15 years ago I received salvation. When I first heard about forgiveness I didn't get it. It took me a few years and a lot of explanations for me to get the whole forgiveness idea.

I forgave everyone although I did have trouble forgiving this sister. She had abused me in every way except sexually. But, through many attempts and with the help of the Holy Spirit I did forgive her.

However, I did not feel any better about her after I did forgive her. I thought perhaps my heart condition was not right. I can't even begin to tell you how many hundreds of times, literally, I forgave her. I did not feel better. I still held onto hatred in my heart.

I didn't know what the missing link was but I knew there was a missing link.

For a few years at least, I had been praying for the Lord to teach me, show me, let me know what it is that I am not doing or was doing wrong. The answer finally came on Nov 12th of this year when you were talking about mercy.

Two sentences that you said changed my life. "Jesus shows us Mercy. We are to show each other Mercy."

<u>That was it!!</u>

That was the missing link.

I went into my prayer closet and contemplated this

and prayed about it. I forgave my sister again but this time I added Mercy into the equation. I realized that I never knew and I still do not know what was going on in her head and in her heart for her to have done what she did to me.

We are still not best friends but at least now I have been and can be in her presence without my stomach being in knots. Now I can even honestly and sincerely tell her I love her.

Laurie

Sharon

"Thank you Lord for allowing me to know that in You I find my strength.

I love You for allowing me to know the real Jesus, the Jesus that lifted me up when I was broken down.

In You Lord I found wholeness through Your Gospel."

Sharon

Cregg

Every day I can sense more awareness of Who

Jesus is and what He stands for. I cherish every day I live as a gift from God and I am so grateful that at any time via the radio, ipod or internet I can hear an encouraging word from you. The days are countless that over and over again I have been uplifted and encouraged through this ministry and what it represents... Jesus.

This past Christmas Seminar you brought forth a message called "The Word Made Flesh." You shared about how Jesus tasted death for all of us. This was one of the areas I struggled in. I used to torment myself on how it's going to be when I take my final breath in this life. Well after hearing that message I see now that, if God can save me from the condition I was in, He can surely handle anything. This is one of the many principles I have learned from this ministry like; living in the present moment and that God has got my past, future and present all covered.

I can go on and on proclaiming all the many holy principles I've learned from this ministry. Ministering to the Lord, taking the lower seat and not seeing how bad I am but how good God is are principles that are placed deep into my heart as I walk in the Lord day in and day out.

I am forever humbled with the fact that God is a loving God and I can live a life in Him without condemnation. Through the 13 blessed years I have been listening I can truly say that the scales of torment have fallen off of me after years of failure and thinking I could never have a relationship with God. Regardless of what goes on in my life I have a true well of joy in my heart overflowing with love and gratitude to Jesus.

Cregg

7

WITH CHILDLIKE FAITH

Michael
(& *Jhayana*)

Jhayana and I love to listen at 3 o clock, Monday - Friday, to "Let's Talk About Jesus."

Hallelujah. Praise the Lord Jesus Christ!

Before 3 o clock on WMCA, Jhayana, at four years of age, is preparing to dance, rejoice, sing, celebrate and laugh with joy when "Let's Talk About Jesus" comes on the air. Thank you! My healing is from the Lord Jesus Christ.

One day I was under some attack of the enemy. Before 3 o clock, I was leaving to go to the doctors for therapy.

Jhayana stopped me from going. She pleaded - "Let's listen to the radio! Let's Talk About Jesus!"

With lowly spirit I agreed. I sat with Jhayana. With childlike faith we listened.

During that Friday program, you read our letter over the radio. WOW!

WOW!

WOW! The love of God fell on us!

Jhayana and I celebrated. Filled with the Holy Spirit, the day was full of joy.

Please pray for Jhayana. Also pray for this Grandfather Michael who wants her to serve the Lord with her gifts and talents. Also God's protection on her life. She loves the Lord. She's listening to God's Word about two years.

When I listen to "Let's Talk About Jesus" it encourages me to go on in life. The light of God comes through the radio. Praise God. Thanks!

Michael

8

SAVED
By Messiah

Elliot

<small>December</small> 30, 2009

I was born "under the law" and raised in the Jewish tradition and heritage. At the time, I did not know just how great that heritage was, but pursuing a scientific career I did have plenty of curiosity, and wanted to know more about this Jew named Jesus.

I began looking into the New Testament and listening to "Let's Talk About Jesus" on the radio. Eventually, I came to understand that everything Jewish people hope for had already taken place - better and more wonderfully than we had ever hoped or imagined!

The Jewish Messiah HAS come; our sins HAVE been forgiven and the love of God IS being poured out upon us and in us continuously to this day and forever.

My question is how so many Jewish people can read their Holy Scriptures and still miss the point. There IS the Messiah - on page after page of the Old

<small>54</small>

Testament... and He is glorious!

Behold - the Lord Jesus Christ stands at the door and knocks. Every day, open that door, seek the promised love, joy, peace and forgiveness of God. Keep that door open every day.

Your brother in Christ, Elliot

⟜

June 28, 2010

Your consistent message and spirit have proven vital over the years. With your help, my Jewish background actually made it easier for me to recognize and believe in the prophetic, Messianic salvation provided by Christ.

As you often point out, Christ is prominently and abundantly featured throughout the Old Testament. With your help, I began to understand Judaism in ways that had never been addressed in Hebrew School.

My greatest Stumbling block was The Trinity.

After all, practicing Jews recite a prayer every morning and evening called the "Shema" - This prayer, recited also at many other important times, states first and above all that, "The Lord is our God, The Lord is one" (a quote of Moses in Deuteronomy 6:4). It is a powerful declaration of faith in the unity of God. Amen.

But what of The Trinity?

Well, it was a slow process, but you have led me to see the wonderful reconciliation to be found in Scripture. With awe and beauty, the Old Testament continues to be revealed in the light of the unity of Christ Jesus. Especially when Jesus Himself prays for ALL believers (near the end of John 17) that we might all be one with Christ in the Father, and He in us. Jesus prays that we may be brought to perfect unity. Hallelujah! Indeed, "The Lord is our God, The Lord is one." Problem solved!

Our Lord not only wants unity, He IS unity! When we are in spiritual fellowship and communion with Him, we ARE one. Thank you for providing the context, meaning and love to get me and so many others through to the truth of eternal life in Christ Jesus, our Messiah.

I urge all who have an ear to hear; the rewards are eternal.

Your brother in Christ, Elliot

∞

JUNE 30, 2011

Over the years Loving Grace Ministries has been lovingly compared to many things, but on Tuesday you said that you were "running out of analogies."

Here's one that might be new: A portable GPS (or global positioning system).

My personal journey began with a Jewish background, but no matter where one begins, without guidance it seems inevitable that you end up lost. I traveled down my road for a long time before even realizing that I was lost... deeply lost.

But then there was a voice... your voice. Not a GPS, but a JPS (or JESUS Positioning System). Your voice said that I was headed in the wrong direction and that I needed to make a U-turn (only you called it repenting).

The new route was quite unexpected. Sometimes I got sidetracked, but your voice would consistently, faithfully, lovingly guide me back to Jesus.

Like a GPS voice, with unending patience, my Jesus positioning System would sometimes say "you've gone too far," "you haven't gone far enough," "you're making a wrong turn," or "Do not turn aside to the right or to the left. Turn your foot from evil" (Proverbs 4:27).

Jesus said "I am the way." What better directions could ever be given?

The JPS is simple: Jesus is always at the center. He always guides us toward home. He is our permanent destination. Over the years your voice has always encouraged us to hear His voice from within, through the Holy Spirit... thus making the Jesus Positioning System portable and perpetual. And, like a GPS system, which gets its information from satellites above, we get our message from heaven above.

We live in a lost world. We all need to let this JPS guide our hands on the steering wheel as we travel down the road of life.

Keep giving out the directions that help to "make straight the way of the Lord" (Isaiah 40:3, John 1:23).

Your brother in Christ, Elliot

Rose

I've been in Israel since November and should be home by January 20, 2010. It is always a joy to come and visit with family, grandchildren and friends, many of whom are believers in The Messiah. The grandchildren are being raised to know The Lord, and little Ellynoam (1 1/2 years) loves to sing Kumbayah my Lord, Kumbayah. So precious. They sing many songs in Hebrew which is the language the boys (Aviel & Ethan, pronounced Aytan) are learning in Gan (pre-school for toddlers).

My son-in-law Mordechai, along with others, is a trainer and facilitator of Seminars dedicated to Leadership of Yeshua training, to young Israeli leaders with the purpose of them going back to their congregations, places of business and market places, training and encouraging others in Him and His Leadership. There is definitely a hunger amongst Israelis who are coming to know the Lord and those who already know Him to follow His Ways and Walk closer to Him everyday.

The gatherings between Israelis and Arab believers (whether of Christian background or former Muslims) is a strong desire to worship The Lord together... something unfortunately you do not hear much of in the world news.

I recently participated in an Arab/Israeli Women's meeting where we sang worship songs together, read from the Scriptures and prayed, all in Arabic, Hebrew and English. We then shared our personal stories, followed by a guest speaker (who lives in the village where my daughter Meira lives).

I recall having moved from upstate New York, to

Tenafly, New Jersey many years ago and I was blessed one day to turn on the radio and hear a young minister speak "All About Jesus." He shared many, many truths about Jesus with a heart filled with so much love for the Lord that it entered into his voice through the airwaves and spoke to my heart in such a Spirit of Unity. What joy it was to later on go to your Evangelical meetings in New York City, whereby "in person" The Family of God met face to face and worshipped and rejoiced in The Lord in Spirit and Truth. Baruch HaShem, Bless His Holy Name.

And much later on, what a privilege it was to bring my daughters and nephew on different occasions to your various weekend retreats where they received The Lord. God Bless you and thank you for choosing to follow The Lord and bless so many, including members of my family. My nephew died, but not without talking about your music that so blessed Him, and the recognition of your humility before Christ, and your courage and strength to fight the good fight... your life testimony helped him to deal with his personal struggles, following Christ to the Cross and receiving His Resurrected Life.

Inside Him, I send my love, til we see each other face to face.

Rose

9

DELIVERED
From Legalism

Nelson

Greetings in the Precious Name of Our Lord and Saviour Jesus Christ. I can't but all the more emphasize "That God Loves Us."

I was born again into a legalistic movement of the mid 80's. I loved my brothers and sisters in the Lord, but the message of the gospel was wrong. It was more about a performance oriented Christianity than a grace oriented one. It was all about what you had to do to please God. I couldn't see the Truth of the Word of God because it was like hidden from me and as a result of this I felt lifeless. I finally walked away from this movement because I felt I had nothing more to give.

My biggest mistake was that I was giving and giving but I wasn't receiving and you can't give of what you don't have.

It was when I started to listen to the "Let's Talk About Jesus" program on the radio that the Holy Spirit quickened a hunger in my life for the Word of God and my eyes were opened to see Our Precious Saviour Jesus Christ come alive as He really is revealed through the Holy Bible.

It was God who gave me a chance to life again through your ministry. Your precious message of The Gospel has a special way of expressing this to the world and all those who listen.

As I mentioned in a previous letter I wrote, the way the Holy Spirit uses you in lifting up Our Lord and Saviour through the steadfast and consistent teachings of the Word of God throughout all these years has taught me that our faith is strengthened by giving Glory to God because with Him all things are possible.

God has done many miracles in my life but the greatest of these was when He saved me and eventually opened my eyes to see Our Precious Saviour JESUS, full of Grace and Truth.

"Praise the Lord God Almighty."

Your Brother in Christ, Nelson

Patricia

Thank you for your card and kind and encouraging words concerning the home-going of my Harry. His passing from this life to his heavenly home was in answer to my prayers and those of family and friends.

The dreadful illness that ended Harry's physical life was sudden and devastating. Our dear Lord was so gracious to take him home and release us from the heartbreak of seeing both his mind and body crumbling on a daily basis.

His loss, after 55 years of marriage, is deeply felt. But Jesus has kept His promise to never leave or forsake me and I rest in the precious hope that we will be reunited in God's time.

It was on your first Saturday broadcast into the Philadelphia area those many years ago, that I found your ministry. I was turning the dial from one religious station to another when I heard a voice say, "Let's Talk About Jesus." I quickly turned back and found the liberating teaching needed by my spirit.

I was raised in the strict legalism of the 40's and 50's. I had lived a life of trying to do the right thing, and not doing the wrong one.

But my spirit was restless for something more.

A friend gave me a copy of "The Cross and the Switchblade" and I began to read the writings of some Christian women who, through the Spirit, showed me that the "something more" was a personal relationship with Jesus unlike any that I had experienced up to that point in my Christian life.

I had accepted the Lord when I was ten years old, and now here I was in my forties finally getting to know the Jesus who had loved me with the Cross, and now lived to have fellowship with me.

And then, just at the right time, along came Loving Grace Ministries. Since, at that time, I was working, I couldn't wait for Saturdays to listen together with Harry, and learn from God's Word the liberating truth of what Jesus accomplished for me at Calvary.

It was all Him.

It was the love of the Father, through the Son, made real to my heart by the Spirit through your teaching and counseling.

The Word became a love letter to me and I was set free from legalistic bondage. Harry joined me along the way in finding this wonderful freedom in a Spirit-filled walk with the Lord.

Your teaching and counseling guided and helped me as I taught a women's class for many years, and then a bi-monthly women's Bible study in my later years. You helped me to show them the wonder of the Word of God as an awesome and beautiful revelation of Jesus Christ.

Your counseling ministry helped me to counsel and guide women to look for Jesus in whatever their circumstance, and to seek to experience His reality as I had learned to do with the help of "Let's Talk About Jesus."

Your faithful teaching concerning the person of Jesus Christ came into our home, helped Harry and I to grow up in the knowledge of the Lord Jesus, and then reached out to family, friends, church family, neighbors and strangers. It has been multiplied over and over again.

Patricia

Jon

LGM has been a blessed source of planting and watering in my life, which our Lord has used to cause the growth.

I received Jesus through a very fearful, legalistic message, and my first couple of years as a believer were laden with heart-wrenching and mind twisting religion, as I sought to please God with my life.

Then one day, after crying out to God the night before in despair and surrender, I turned on the radio and heard the glorious message of the Gospel of grace through LTAJ.

It was that day that I truly met the Lord Jesus Christ in the fullness of His true Gospel. I felt a joy and peace and freedom that truly is "beyond comprehension."

Sometimes the thoughts of God's true-character which I've received through your teaching over the years are the very things that help me make it through another day. I hate to think of where I would be if our Father had not revealed to me His grace, His Beloved Son Jesus.

Your bro in Him, Jon

∝

JUNE 22, 2011

I thank and praise my Father for all He has done

in my life.

I first committed my life to the Lord through much fear and with much confusion. The first couple of years of my life were lived in terrible legalism and bondage (which I'm still rooting out today). But at my greatest point of desperation God led me to LTAJ and revealed to me the true Gospel of His love and grace in Jesus Christ.

That day I was set free from the chains of guilt and fear that bound me, and I am forever grateful. I am blessed. I pray that more lives would experience the saving and liberating truth of Jesus.

In Jesus' name, Jon

10

THERE WAS
SOMETHING MISSING

Trudy

DECEMBER 11, 2009

I only started listening about three months ago. I had never heard of you. Your radio program has touched my heart deeply and I am very grateful.

I am now 49 years of age and have been trying to follow Jesus to the best of my ability since I was 27 years old. But I always felt there was something missing. And I really don't know exactly what that was. All I know is that since I have been listening to you I feel spiritually and psychologically better.

You have brought me back to simplicity and I have never felt the love of Jesus as much as I have since I have been listening to you. You have put a lot of things in perspective for me. The Bible has become so interesting to me now since Jesus has put you in my path. I leave work at 3:00pm and I dash to my car because I look so forward to listening to you and learning.

You even make my spiritual life fun. I never thought of Jesus as being fun. But you have made it fun for me to learn about Him. If anything, I have always viewed Jesus as a harsh judge with scowling eyebrows. But you have changed that image and I thank you for that. That other image that I struggled with has only caused me problems.

God bless you and thank you again.

Trudy

DECEMBER 16, 2009

God Bless you and thank you for sharing my letter of testimony on the air. I really appreciate that.

I thank God every day for this radio program "Let's Talk About Jesus." I have had enlightenments and I really would like to share with you one of them that has been having a profound effect on my spiritual life.

A little while back, not too long ago, you taught about how to pray, or how to enter prayer. It went something like this from what I remember. "When you pray to God, remember Who you are praying to, and praise Him and thank Him first before making your requests known."

Well, I started doing this and it is bringing about wonderful results and good fruit. First of all, I would like to say this. I don't want to sound like everything is all wonderful now and life is great and I have no more problems. If anything, I still have the same problems and issues. But the difference is profound for me. I followed your suggestion on how to enter prayer; I praise Jesus and thank Him first for all of His wonderful Blessings to me. I tell God how much I love Him and spend some time worshipping Him first. I do this for a few minutes, and you are right, after awhile I forget about what I wanted to ask Him in the first place.

This way of entering prayer has completely taken the focus off of me and my problems and has put the focus back on Jesus where it belongs. I am experiencing a connection with God that I have not felt in a very long time due to this. It humbles me and reminds me that I am very little. It helps me to let go of my problems and puts me in a very relaxed state of mind knowing that I am turning it over to God and trusting that He is going to take care of everything. It takes the pressure off of me.

And most of all, this way of praying has given me a HAPPY HEART! I thank God for this wonderful enlightenment.

Trudy

$\propto$

DECEMBER 24, 2009

After being saved 22 years ago, I thought I knew Jesus. But I really didn't. It is only after listening to this wonderful program that I am finally getting to know Him.

I feel peace in my soul.

There are quite a few things that I have really learned. One of them, which has been profound for me, is this: I always thought the goal was to reach some kind of an emotion. If I did feel that high emotion, I thought I was close to Jesus. If I didn't feel that high, and was down in a valley and going through a dry spell, that meant I wasn't close to Jesus.

I have learned through this program to be realistic. I have come to see that it is through faith and believing in the Gospel **THE TRUE WAY** that this is <u>the way</u> to stay close to Jesus.

I don't depend on my emotions anymore. This has been such an eye opener, and I cannot stress enough that is has been psychologically healing for me.

I thank God everyday for this.

Trudy

$\propto$

JUNE 2, 2010

I was saved in 1987 after my brother had passed away. During my walk I always struggled with feeling the presence of Jesus in my life. No matter how many works of service I did, I still somehow never really felt His presence.

Well one day I thought to myself, if I just decorated our home with a lot of religious art, knicknacks and statues, I just might feel more of Our Lord's presence. This went on for years. Not that there is anything wrong with having religious items around, I don't want to make anyone feel bad about that; that is not my intention.

About a month before I started listening to "Let's Talk About Jesus," I was feeling extremely disappointed, disheartened and quite confused. I started to remove all of my religious items, pictures and statues and just packed them away. I didn't know why I was doing this. I also was not feeling moved to do any kind of service. I thought at first God was angry with me. This was all so disturbing. It was like God was pulling me away from everything. I was saying to myself, "Now why would I want to remove my religious items, surely our Lord would want me to keep them around."

I started listening to "Lets' Talk About Jesus," and I cannot express enough the blessing that was outpoured on me at this time. God was so determined to help me feel His powerful presence on His terms. Through this radio program, God led me to HIS WORD! There is just not enough to say about this. The gratitude that I have is overwhelming.

I am enjoying Our Lord's presence so much. When I come home from work, there are no religious items around, but God is there waiting to greet me and wrap His arms around me when I walk through that door. I JUST KNOW IT!!!

I thank God everyday for this. God bless you!
Trudy

11

HEALED
God's Healing Presence

Michael

I am a listener of only about 2 years now and am about to celebrate my first year of my new life in Christ.

In 2009 I thought I lost almost everything. I was completely broken of spirit after dealing with some difficult circumstances, as well as financial difficulties. In my darkest hours when I even contemplated suicide, I broke down and handed my life over to Jesus.

I reached for Him and He reached back.

He made His presence known to me in a way I had never dreamed possible and in an instant He comforted me. He took all of the pain and anxiety I was feeling away. I have never felt such an overwhelming feeling of love and acceptance and comfort.

From that day on my life has changed, I know that He has given me a new life in Him and I am living that life to please Him.

I used to live to please others and myself and I know what that got me.

My eyes have been opened to the truth and the truth has indeed set me free! Listening to your show as well as reading my Bible and spending time with some people that God placed in my life for a short time all helped get me to where I am now.

I thought I lost everything in 2009 but the truth is I have gained everything. I wake up every day now and just feel so blessed and so fortunate that I belong to Jesus.

Michael

Win

This morning I read the entire book of Colossians and as I was reading I saw so clearly that your intent, your struggle is the same that the apostle Paul had - to keep the body of Christ intact in Him, (Christ). To keep us from looking anywhere but to Christ. To not be drawn away to human reasonings about the things of God, but to solely look to Jesus and stay put.

Because you preach and teach only Jesus, the entire bible (which I've been reading for 36 years) finally "all" makes sense to me now. It has come together for me like a hand in a glove and what a delight to pick it up, read the words of life and understand them!

Because of your faithful teaching of Jesus Christ, I no longer try to go around Him and enter God's presence through the 'back door' - I now go straight to Christ with my eyes only on Him and let me tell you a whole new

heavenly vista has opened up to me!
In His everlasting love, Win

John

Our Bible study group started 19 months ago using Wayne's tapes, beginning with Galatians and now studying Ministering unto the Lord. Frankly, as a lifelong Catholic who has always believed in God, this has now changed my life and I now have a personal relationship with Jesus which has totally enhanced my faith and is making me more aware of His presence even in the difficult tribulations in the material world.

God Bless, John

Benjamin

"Let's Talk About Jesus" has brought a lot of clearness to my thinking about what I should dwell on. I praise God that He has revealed the most important things to give our attention to. Like Jesus is the center of our life and we live in the New Testament days, not the Old

Testament days. Bless God also for the peace of mind this brings to our thirsty souls. "Thou will keep him in perfect peace whose mind is stayed on Thee" (Isaiah 26:3).

Benjamin

John C.

Very few ministers that I hear seek Jesus in the Scriptures as you have taught us and if not for you I may have never heard that this was possible. Everyone needs to build their relationship with Jesus by seeing Him all throughout the Scriptures. I believe you said we will be learning of Jesus for all eternity so why not start seeking Him and learning of Him now? I can hear you say about Jesus, "learn of Me." Thank you for being an important part of my personal relationship with Jesus.

Your brother in Christ, John

Karen

When I was 8 years old I prayed the prayer of salvation - I accepted the Lord. On July 9th, 2003, 35 years later, I met my Savior. For the first time in my walk with Him, I knew I was truly saved.

It was through a constant message of personal relationship with a Living God through Loving Grace that I finally saw the Light. I can't explain it all - I only know that living in the unadulterated walk of the New Covenant that Christ died for, is indeed Life.

Through some very difficult seeking years, Wayne spoke of something that I really wanted - not religion, not programs - something real that didn't require my maintenance. He bore a testimony of the truth that Christ desires to live in us, love us, help us through this crazy world we live in. And 8 years further down the road, I see His hand in everything that is good in my life - I'm not searching and programming - He is with me.

I think singly the thing that brought this to life for me was the beautiful teaching of being a priest unto Him that Wayne faithfully supplies. It is so easy-yet we miss it - and that seems to be the way in.

If you are seeking, you will find Him. And don't give up until you are fully satisfied with what you have with Him. Just keep seeking. Cultivate your priesthood - it's beautiful.

I am indebted to Loving Grace for helping me find Jesus.

Karen

12

SET FREE
In Prison

"I was in prison and you came to Me."
Jesus, Matthew 25:36

Terrance

JUNE 1, 2010

I first started to listen to your broadcast in January and since then you've been a major inspiration towards the complete understanding of "The Love of Jesus Christ"...in my life.

I find myself in a new life, new heart, new mind, and most of all a new creation.

I was once under the lifestyle of corruption and darkness guiding myself into damnation. However that was then and feeding off the love of Christ is now. I find myself understanding the power of prayer, and now living in a constant conversation with God. My blessings arise to new levels as I continue to decrease, allowing Him to increase.

I've also learned to see the devil as he approaches. Discerning right from wrong and dressing myself daily with the Armor of God, and passing the burden to Him... I am a major player right now and I would like to keep it that way. I am able to envision myself in the plan that He has for me. However I <u>need more</u>!

I wish to excel in the Word of God, and become a blessing to others. There is a lot to be learned and I hear you say that you've been saved for 30 something years, and you're still learning.

Well Wayne you and the continuation of your ministry is forever in my prayers. God bless and may the Love of Christ live in us <u>All.</u>

Terrence

June 15, 2010

My spirit is overwhelmed with a joyous feeling from your program. It has delivered the inspiration of Wanting to know My Lord and personal Savior personally.

At this point and time I am residing in a correctional facility on charges that kept my mind occupied upon a wave of negative thinking, and lacking much of the hope that is required to keep faith alive in all circumstances. So with my back against the wall I decided to transition my life from the darkness to the light... And by the grace of God that transition is "<u>Complete</u>"! I needed a way out

Spiritually, so I turned my full attention to the <u>will</u> of my Father, and accepting the "Sacrifical Lamb" and His spotless blood as my <u>Salvation</u>!

Through your program I now understand that "it is no longer I who live; but Christ lives in me; and the life which I now live in the flesh I live by faith in the son of God" (Galatians 2:20). Allowing myself to scoot over and allowing Him to drive, willing and decreasing daily to do His will at the cost of Dying Daily for His will to be done within me as the "vessel" and becoming "complete in Him, who is the Head of all principality" (Colossians 2:10).

By the Grace of God I would love to endure the continuance of the inspiration that has been delivered from your ministry. The enlightenment of your bringing me closer to the "LORD" is so that I can learn to "stand fast in the liberty by which Christ has made us free" (Galatians 5:1).

I knew that a tree is known by its fruits; "either make the tree good and its fruit good or else make the tree bad and its fruit bad," and this is the teaching of your ministry that my Spirit eagerly awaits each day. I thank you for the deliverance of a beautiful word, and giving hope, peace, knowledge, brotherly love, passion, experience, and guidance to my faith, understanding and spirit.

"For I can do all things through Christ Jesus who strengthens me" (Philippians 4:13).

Terrance

*W*ilmer

Greetings in the name of our Lord and Savior Jesus Christ our soon coming King. My name is Wilmer and I am currently incarcerated at Riker's Island.

Every day at 3pm we listen to "Let's Talk About Jesus" on WMCA 570 am. There is a group of us that study together. At 3pm we are locked in for count and with only 3 radios and 11 of us we take turns. Whoever ones have the radio takes notes and teach for the evening class. Praise God.

Most of the men I am teaching are 23-49 years of age. They call me "Pops." Your program has blessed us because it has brought unity on the block.

Each day we thank God. I am facing 18 months but mostly the others much, much more. I really wish to leave here knowing that I have done something in serving the Lord.

Respectfully & sincerely in Christ,
Wilmer

*R*obin

Let me introduce myself, my name is Robin. I am a 48 year old male, currently incarcerated at Metropolitan Detention Center in Brooklyn. I have about 14 months left on my sentence. I plead guilty to conspiracy to import and smuggle counterfeit wearing apparel from China.

I want to thank you for your radio program. A small (10 inmates) group of us listen to your program from 3pm to 4pm and we discuss on Tuesday and Thursday prayer meetings. Your program is an uplifting program. The music touches my heart! We know that we have broken the law, we are doing our time, reading and studying the Word of God! Prison is sometimes the best thing for a person like me, as I knew the Word, tried to follow it but I lived on the fence. Now I am here, getting my life back together! Getting my family back! I had everything when I was on the streets - money - women - drugs - friends, but I had no God. I lost everything, but, GOD NEVER LEFT ME! For this I am grateful.

Wayne keep up what you are doing. There are many people here who are broken and beaten, but with the Word of God there is liberty.

Robin

John

JULY 2, 2010

I listen and pray with you. Your program has been such a blessing for me and other brothers here at Rahway. Your program is so enlightening and the Spirit of God speaks to my heart that your program is the true message of the Gospel - Jesus! The Lord is moving mightily here at Rahway Prison (East Jersey State Prison) and there are some spirit filled brothers here and I know they listen to you and benefit from the Bread of Life. People look down on prisoners, but what or where a better place to have the Spirit of Jesus coming into hearts of broken souls and regenerating, washing, and filling with His Love. I will continue to pray daily for your ministry. In the love of Christ Jesus,

John

P.S. Thank you so much for books! God bless you!

SEPTEMBER 3, 2010

I truly am blessed by your program on 570am, WMCA 3-4pm, M-F. I am coming up on one year since I got on my knees and confessed my sins and Jesus Christ as my Lord and Savior and you've helped me to search the Scriptures and learn that He is my High Priest and I am a priest unto Him.

I've been in prison for 16+ years now and was so against God and felt so abandoned and hurt. We all have a history and I hope mine will one day be a blessing to help keep people out of prison and alcohol abuse. But I won't go into that now.

I just want to share that I wake up and my first thought is "Thank You Lord!" I used to rue every morning! But praise Jesus I am grateful and I believe all I've gone through is for the good of His purpose and when He is ready to let me go I am excited to be used.

I used to be an opponent to Jesus, reading books to bring into question that whole gamut of anti-Jesus info.

Then last September my mother had heart surgery and my friend got cancer and someone said to pray for them. I took their suggestion and read the bible with an open mind and heart. And Praise Him! The Holy Spirit moved on me and I have been daily in the Word and Prayer and repented of my sin. I've been empowered by the Holy Spirit to go from 40 cigarettes a day to 0 for about 10 months now and got rid of porn and cussing and I'm blessed with some wonderful brothers in Christ which includes you, that encourage me daily.

I just want to praise Him and thank you and all at the ministry for sharing the Bread of Life just as my Bible and Holy Spirit confirms. Amen.

DECEMBER 14, 2011

I've been listening to your radio program for around two years now. My spiritual birthday is September 10th, 2009. I'm 44 years old and in my 18th year in prison. 2 1/2 years ago if you said I'd be writing this letter I... well let's just say it wouldn't have been any blessings coming out of my mouth.

But God!

Jesus Christ, my Lord and Savior, left glory to

come down to this fallen human infested planet to lay down His life for us all and shed His pure and precious blood. And I am still in awe, just past two years since Jesus revealed Himself to me.

The Holy Spirit has strengthened my inner man to peel the layers of "protection" back that I've had, and have the love of God poured into me. I am so thankful and grateful for this love and a peace and joy deep within that I know you know. I am in God's hand and nothing can pluck me out. The Holy Spirit has put assurance inside of me that I can be a vessel, a slave to righteousness for I've certainly been a slave and prisoner of unrighteousness. I know I have a long way to go, but the love and mercy I know, "Jesus," makes me want to honor God for the privilege of allowing me to be a minister of reconciliation.

My earliest memory of my father was of him sexually abusing me as he beat me with a wire brush. These are the only memories I have of that man. My mom replaced him with a six foot four, two hundred eighty pound biker with a beard down to his belly, an alcoholic who didn't sexually abuse me, but close fist beat me until I was eleven to twelve and ran away. The constant physical abuse and torment of screaming, having to watch my mom get beat and often raped and trying to help her, which only brought worse beatings, culminated one night after he smashed a large mug on the side of my head. I got out and ran until I couldn't run any longer. It was snowing I was in a pair of jeans and t-shirt and sneakers.

A car stopped, an older man and a warm car, and I stepped into a world that I wouldn't wish on anyone. A predator with many predator friends in and around NYC led to drugs and prostitution before High School even began.

My stepdad would go to jail and the psych-ward for periods of time and I'd go back and forth from mom to the predators. I was in and out of rehabs and A.A. and N.A. and lost in a "prison" within myself of shame and hate and sorrow.

I hated myself and I hated God. I did believe there was a God and I believed if I killed myself I would go to a place for eternity and be stuck with everyone who killed themselves and I would have to listen to them whine forever. I "know" many have had worse lives than me, but without getting too into it, going from the violence of "home," to the "sickness," to running away from "that," to abandoned buildings on the lower east side - I've seen death, sickness and darkness most couldn't fathom.

So I existed, trying to function in the world while trying to hide and be numb; going to rehabs, to jail, to prison.

Though I didn't commit murder but helped try to cover one up, prison potentially saved me from eventually killing someone in a bar fight or driving drunk into a wall or worse.

At 26, my 35 year sentence seemed like "forever," so I spent many years in the beginning scarring myself with angry tattoos, fighting any and all, and spending months upon months in the hole. I studied anti-Christian material and spent my time locked within the "prison" within myself of hurt, shame, and anger as I was just doing time. I mellowed some with age but was still steeped in sin.

Two plus years ago my mom was having serious heart problems and my friend Joanne was experiencing very bad health problems so I asked this guy Dave to pray for them. I used to argue with him at how the Bible was all contradictions and God was no good. But Dave kept praying for me, showing me Jesus, wondering why God sent this angry white guy to his cell door.

But Praise Jesus! The Holy Spirit led him to suggest "I" pray for them and I said I couldn't. He said I should maybe try to read the Bible and, with an open heart and mind, try to learn about the God of love and grace and mercy, and <u>then</u> pray for my people, though he would pray too.

So I snuck a Bible to my cell and since my name is John I started reading John and Praise Jesus when I finished his Gospel it was revealed to me that Jesus was my Savior and died for me and it wasn't <u>His</u> fault, but <u>sin</u>'s fault for the life I had.

I got to my knees and, crying a long cry I needed so bad, I asked Jesus to be my Lord, and I believed He is my Savior.

I was so joyed to tell Dave the next day! I got baptized here at Rahway on October 11th, 2009 and have been growing from grace to grace in the grace and knowledge of Jesus. I have been blessed with a hunger for the Word and the Holy Spirit is working mightily in me and as I said earlier I have a long way to go, but right away the porn "pollution" and cussing God was removed. God removed smoking from me in January 2010 after 30+ years.

By the blood of Jesus Christ I actually have a peace within. I feel cleansed from the stain of the past, and I am actually praying for the many that caused the hurt, though almost all are passed on, so it's just for the spirit of forgiveness.

I know there are many in here that are lost in that darkness I was in and don't believe they can find change.

But Jesus Christ pierced through the layers of pain and shined light into my spirit, soul, and body. I've received His love. I can say I love You Abba "Father," a word that made me cringe inside. But now I can spiritually put my hand in His and trust Him and yield and submit myself to His Holy Spirit to lead me through each moment.

There is a Holy Spirit led bunch of men here and it's growing, praise Jesus. Jesus has blessed us to search the Holy Scriptures daily, to present ourselves wholly to Him, our reasonable service (Romans 12:1). And we Praise Jesus for His love, mercy, and cleansing comfort.

But God!

I must decrease. He must increase. Jesus Christ is my High Priest and ministering unto the Lord has been blissful. The other day when you were playing a worship tape I just began to worship and God blessed me with such joy and when I sort of came back to the program you were just quoting from Isaiah 61:7... "everlasting joy shall be theirs." The first line in my NKJV says, "Instead of your shame you shall have double honor." Praise Jesus. Ephesians 5:8 says, "For you were once darkness, but now you are light in the Lord. Walk as children of light." Those are like cleansing words pouring over me from the Fountain of Refreshing. I know I am truly loved by the One True Father, the Mighty Counselor, the Prince of Peace. It is a delight to bless Him daily.

I've been dealing with a knee problem for almost four years but since being saved it has become a blessing being able to witness while out on medical trips to guys from other prisons, however the Spirit leads me. I'm learning Spanish and that will open up a whole world of witnessing.

When I get out in November 2016, God willing, I

hope to be able to go by the power of the Holy Spirit to bring light to wherever He wills me to go.

If Jesus can shine His light into my darkness, then as it speaks of in 2 Corinthians 1:3-7, my comfort from God concerning past afflictions can be to His glory in expanding His Kingdom. I have a fear and reverence for God, not man, and hope to be a vessel, an ambassador, a minister of reconciliation to the glory of Christ Jesus. I'm just His humble servant. Truly to God be all the glory.

Thank you Jesus for the love that is the greatest gift. My prayer is for us all to grow and come to the unity of the faith and of the knowledge of the Son of God, to a perfect man, to the measure of the stature of the fullness of Christ (Ephesians 4:13). Amen.

Bless the Lord! God bless you all. Thank you my brothers and sisters.

In the love of Christ Jesus, John

A1

I know this, that in Jesus Christ everything is yes. Anything else is not the Gospel. So here I am, six years into a seven year stretch at a New York State prison. I am so blessed in the Lord I cannot stop bringing every thought captive to Christ. Even when I wrote the word "stretch" a few lines before my spirit automatically starts blessing the Lord Christ for "stretching" out on the cross.

For the past few years I've had a steady, redundant diet of the Full Gospel as preached by you. But now something has happened. My spirit crossed the line and won't go back, meaning this - I am Understanding, Believing, but now <u>Am Experiencing</u> My relationship with God in such a way that nothing else is desirable or makes any sense. I've always had this awareness but now the river is flowing. I see it now and have jumped right in.

These past few months have been indescribable. I just sit here for 5, 6, 8 hours and dive into the Scriptures or just sit or minister and we conversate and His presence just blesses my head off!

I could go on about Jesus forever. My prayer is that we all simply go on about Jesus forever.

Do as the Bible says, come eat, thirsty drink, be alone with God. Be alone with God; He will reveal Himself. Bury yourself in Christ. Sit down, listen and receive and listen again, and listen again. God will honor that commitment of you seeking Him out. He will show Himself. I love all at LGM and all my brothers and sisters in Christ.

A prisoner in the flesh but a real prisoner of Jesus Christ .

Love, Al

JR

I'd like to introduce myself. My name is Brother

JR and I am currently incarcerated in the NJ state prison system half way through a 7 year sentence. The "good news" about me being here is that our loving God plucked me out of the mess I was making of my life, and saved me. Although I hate being locked up, (away from my kids, and am ashamed of the hurt my actions caused), I recognize the Lord's powerful and loving hand in all of this.

I have been blessed to have been sent a cassette copy of your recent "Worship in the Woods" by my dear Brother John Scalzo. Although I have been listening to your monthly "Talk About Jesus" message on tape and have been blessed, the message and worship from the worship weekend has had a profound impact on my life.

I can now recognize a calling on my life ever since I was very young. But wanting to live my life my way led me to ignoring the call. It was not until everything was removed from my life that I finally reached up and asked God if it was not too late.

Ever since then my life has had new meaning, even in my current valley experience. I have followed the Lord now for only about 5 years and consider myself still to be a baby. God has used me as a praise and worship leader in this place being I was a professional musician prior to my crime. We have a very active Church ministry in here and I am blessed to be able to share my gifts.

I do read my Bible and have devotional time everyday (once again having the time to do so being locked up, and recognizing it is His Word that is sustaining me).

I want to know Jesus in the truest, purest form. I don't want man's spin on Him and I believe that with the Spirit He has indwelled in me, and my Bible, that this is all

I need.

I appreciate your time in reading this.
JR

Steve

After over 6 years I am happy to report that I am 35 days away from being released from prison. Actually I'm finishing this last portion of my sentence in a Community Release Program. I cannot wait to join a church and worship with a Body of Believers.

One cold February morning 6 years ago, I turned on my radio and listened to your message. I got on my knees late that evening and the next morning a miracle occurred. I woke up, a new man, a renewed man, and with great hope for a future with Jesus.

I see your ministry today as a labor of love. A ministry that has taught me about our AMAZING INHERITANCE, a ministry that has taught me to be still and quiet, and a ministry that's taught me Christmas is about Jesus. I had thought is was about lights, presents, and egg-nog, prior to my conversion. Today I know it's Jesus, our Prince of Peace, our Wonderful Counselor.

God bless you, your entire family, and the ministry.

Your brother in Christ, Steve

13

IT'S ALL ABOUT JESUS

William

MARCH 26, 2010

I've had so much religion stuffed down my throat and tried so hard to please God and thought I'd never make it and was ready to give up. I just wasn't holy enough, didn't know how to pray right, couldn't get all the rules right and didn't fit in at all with those religious folk.

Somehow JESUS found me and I received His love. I heard your broadcast a few weeks back (Experiencing Christ in You #4) and I was shouting amens and hallelujahs.

I get it now.

It's all about JESUS! I don't need another experience by any name. I just need more of JESUS.

I'm just a little baby in CHRIST and that's ok. I'm ok with that today. All I need is to dwell in the Light of God my Savior and let Christ be formed in me. HAL-LE-LU-JAH! Thank you JESUS! I love Him more every day!

He's so wonderful!

$\propto$

JUNE 1, 2010

The love of God has won my heart and broke the chains of fear that had kept me away from God.

I had a desire, and I know I had a need but thought there was no way God could still love me after how thoroughly I'd failed, after walking away from Him some years back. I never - not even back when I was walking with God, really understood His love for me. The Lord used Let's Talk About Jesus to bring me to a deeper, fuller knowledge of Him and of who I am in Him.

I am learning to worship God again and how important it is for me to do that. That's an answer to prayer. If my day is going badly and I am struggling with loneliness, depression and isolation I know I will have at least an hour of fellowship via radio. I have been listening since March and many days have gotten a word from the Lord through your teaching.

There have been several times that L.T.A.Jesus has just totally turned my day around, reminding me, "Oh Yeah! God LOVES me. I'm His child!" (Psalm 42:7).

$\propto$

Dear Brother Wayne,

Maybe you are gettiing tired of hearing from me - well that's just too bad. You'd better get used to me because we'll be spending eternity together!

Brother, I've been on a search. I've been searching for meaning, for belonging, for peace with God and for joy. I read the Bible every day. I attend church. I pray. But it wasn't fulfilling. I knew I was missing something. I was catching glimpses of something better but I was being misled.

From the bottom of my poor, needy heart I want to thank you for introducing me to this JESUS that I never really knew. Praise God!

He's not just the starting point - He is the point!

He's not part of the truth, He is the Truth! He's my TRUTH! He's my Way! HALLELUJAH! Bless the name of Jesus!

I really like what you said about perfect love casting out fear. I think I'm starting to get it! Yes, the fear of God is the <u>beginning</u> of wisdom. That fear shows us our need. The fear of death wakes us up to our problem. But when we come to Christ we move out of that fear and into Him! Hallelujah! What Freedom! I can't write fast enough! Praise God!

God doesn't want us to be afraid of Him does He?

It's <u>HIS</u> perfect <u>LOVE</u> that casts out my fear!

I've been waiting to get made perfect, tarrying long, striving hard to get what He ALREADY Gave! O my JESUS you are so wonderful!

I was warned about preachers like you who

talk about LOVE, GRACE and FREEDOM and about actually <u>enjoying</u> fellowship with God! HA HA!

Here's the revelation! God made me to be me! Took me 45 years to get it, but I get it.

July 26, 2010

I had a really rough day yesterday. I was in (am in) a lot of pain. Old man was raging to get out. Blaming myself, hating myself, doubting myself. Confusion. Loneliness. Despair. Doubting. Crying while I paint. "My tears have been my meat day and night." Feeling like a complete failure. Trying to pray. Asking the Lord for help. Trying to turn my thinking around but kept getting pulled back down.

I asked the Lord, "Please tell me I'm not a complete failure," and immediately I heard Wayne's voice: "Well, you are a failure, get over it" (from a tape, don't know which one) and I had to chuckle a little inside.

Praise God for "BUT NOW."

Praise God for a new creation. Praise God that He doesn't view me as some second class saint because of how far off I'd strayed.

I'm His! I'm washed! I'm clean because of the Word He has spoken to me. I have the mind of Christ! Some put me down by bringing up my past but it's been nailed to the cross. It's dead.

So yesterday afternoon as I was being assaulted

and tempted I stopped and renewed my vows. And I said "I can't wait to get home and get in my secret place before God."

The Lord is my Shepherd. He knows where I've been and where I'm going. He's not done with me yet. I'm walking with JESUS from here on out. My children will know their father loves God with all his heart and will be blessed through me. They know I'm a changed man. I am a new man. Praise God.

I love JESUS more and more every day! He just gets better and better.

JUNE 22, 2011

I've been listening to Let's Talk About Jesus for a little over a year now and Wayne' message of "God's love for all people" has been helping me overcome my poor self image and the guilt of my past sins and failures.

I grew up in a dysfunctional, abusive family. I lost my father when I was 14 to illness. I was neglected. I was sexually abused by one of my sister's boyfriends when I was 17.

I guess it was self-preservation that led me to isolate myself from people. I didn't trust anybody. I never let anyone see the real me.

I found the answer in drugs and alcohol. Over time I didn't even know the real me any longer.

I carried all my baggage into marriage. She put up

with me for 17 years, but my self-destructive, addictive behavior eventually wore her down. We're divorced now.

In the depression, loneliness and despair that followed my divorce I turned to God. The only God I ever knew, from Sunday School and church in my youth, was the rule-giver: the very strict and demanding perfection impersonal God.

So I tried to get on the straight and narrow. I quit all my bad habits, read the Bible studiously, wore the right clothes, went to church 3 times a week (or more), tithed of my income and surrounded myself with people who did the same things.

In trying to become perfect, I became perfectly miserable.

I never could let on how miserable I was because I was supposed to be "in the victory" all the time which meant, I thought, to be always happy and never in need.

What followed was that I got angry at God. I felt like He wasn't living up to His end of the deal. In retrospect I now see that I wasn't truly seeking God at all, I was just trying to manipulate God. Eventually I returned to my old vices.

For a time that cycle continued: Walk as perfectly as I could; get angry at God; return to my sinful habits; repent...

During that time I happened to tune into 560 AM one day. I'll never forget it. Wayne was teaching about "Christ in you, your hope of glory." I never heard a preacher say the kinds of things Wayne said. I wept for the entire hour and from the depth of my being I cried to God. I knew this is what I needed - I knew that this is what's been missing from my walk with God all along.

It wasn't as if God touched me that day and I was

instantly, dramatically changed. It's been slow growing for me. But I am learning to relate to God through Jesus Christ in a new way - through love. I go through times of discouragement and depression and sometimes I feel like giving up. Now I know, thanks to Wayne, that that doesn't mean that God's given up on me!

Today I am drug and alcohol free (including tobacco)! Not because I'm trying to earn God's favor, but because I'm learning to love myself. My body is God's Temple. He chose me as a dwelling place. I should take good care of God's temple.

One of my biggest struggles is fighting off these feelings that I have that God is disappointed with me or angry at me all the time. It's hard to enjoy the presence of God that way. I've learned through Wayne's teaching that God sees me as His beloved child, holy and acceptable. I am clothed with a robe of righteousness.

It's taking me a long time to accept and believe these things because I've had a lifetime of living in self-hatred. I still have times of depression, doubt and discouragement when my "old-man" still wants to run the show. But more and more I am becoming rooted and grounded on the rock of God's Love for me in Jesus Christ.

Thank you and God bless you.

JUNE 30, 2011

I was blind but now I see. God's love is for sinners like me.

The ten most important things I've learned from Pastor Wayne:

1. God's love for me is an incontrovertible fact (I like that word "incontrovertible"!)

2. My true identity is in Jesus Christ, not in how others see me - or even how I see myself.

3. God's love heals my emotions. He cares about my emotions and gives me hope.

4. I can be honest with myself about my sinfulness without hating myself for it - that the "sin problem" is no longer the issue - praise God! Jesus took my sins out of the way when He paid for them with His precious blood at Calvary.

5. Salvation isn't a once and done thing - God has called me to a relationship.

6. I set myself up for a fall if I think I'm going to become perfect all at once. It's a little bit of growth every day.

7. Christ and I are inseparable.

8. Worshipping God is very important.

9. I am holy and beloved and a priest unto God forever.

10. IT'S ALL ABOUT JESUS!

14

SAVED, DELIVERED, HEALED AND SET FREE

You

"This is eternal life, that they may know You, the only true God, and Jesus Christ whom You have sent."

John 17:3

What God has graciously done for others, He is ready to do for you.

Are you ready to let God change you into a new creation?

Have you ever received Jesus Christ as your personal Lord and Savior? Do you desire to have a living relationship with The Living God? God expressed His forgiveness for everyone at the Cross. "God so loved the world that He gave His only begotten Son, that whoever believes in Him shall not perish, but have eternal life" (John 3:16).

"Whosoever shall call upon the name of the Lord shall be saved." Romans 10:13

If you are ready now, pray this simple prayer, from your heart (the words in the prayer don't save you. Jesus saves you. But these words, prayed sincerely, will bring Christ to you).

"Lord God, I open up my heart to You. I ask You to come into my life Jesus. I need and want to be born again. I thank You that You died for my sins at Calvary, which I now confess and give to you. I thank You that You are risen from the dead so that I may live forever with You. Come live in me now Lord Jesus. Thank You for making me Your child. I pray that You will lead me into good fellowship with brothers and sisters in Jesus Christ. Thank You for saving me. In Jesus' Name I pray, Amen."

"If you confess with your mouth that Jesus Christ is Lord, and believe in your heart that God raised Him from the dead, you shall be saved."
Romans 10:9

"On this day (date)_____,
I (your name), _____,
give my life to Jesus Christ, receiving His
indwelling, resurrection Life in return. I turn
from sin to the Living God Who loves me,
gave His life for me, and now lives in me that I
may know Him and walk with Him in love, for
now and forever. Thank You Lord. Amen."

"I thank Christ Jesus our Lord, who has strengthened me, because He considered me faithful, putting me
into service, even though I was formerly a blasphemer and
a persecutor and a violent aggressor.

Yet I was shown mercy because I acted ignorantly
in unbelief; and the grace of our Lord was more than
abundant, with the faith and love which are found in Christ
Jesus.

It is a trustworthy statement, deserving full acceptance, that Christ Jesus came into the world to save sinners, among whom I am foremost of all.

Yet for this reason I found mercy, so that in me as
the foremost, Jesus Christ might demonstrate His perfect
patience as an example for those who would believe in
Him for eternal life.

Now to the King eternal, immortal, invisible, the

only God, be honor and glory forever and ever. Amen."

The Apostle Paul

1st Timothy 1:12-17

Hallelujah... and now begins your own new journey of life in Jesus Christ. God bless you this day, now and forever.